LIVING FRUITFULLY
GENEROSITY

Learning from the Saints

Fr John S Hogan

GW00724581

*All booklets are published thanks
to the generosity of the supporters
of the Catholic Truth Society*

CATHOLIC TRUTH SOCIETY
PUBLISHERS TO THE HOLY SEE

"To give and not to count the cost"
St Ignatius of Loyola

All rights reserved. First published 2018 by The Incorporated Catholic Truth Society 40-46 Harleyford Road London SE11 5AY Tel: 020 7640 0042 Fax: 020 7640 0040 © 2018 The Incorporated Catholic Truth Society.

ISBN 978 1 78469 561 3

Contents

Introduction

There was that moment, as she stood at the threshold, when she could have turned back – back into the convent, the school, the habit, back to her name. But the street stretched out before her, with all its possibilities, fears and sacrifices. Hidden there were the voices silenced by want and despair, and she could not ignore them. For Mother Teresa Gonxhe Bojaxhiu there was an urging in her heart that could not be explained – it was not from her, but from Another. The visions had ended, the light was gone; now darkness had descended, and in that darkness she was to give until there was nothing left. The voice of Christ from the cross, "I Thirst", beckoned from the streets of Calcutta and she stepped out.

The future St Teresa of Calcutta had made the decision to lift the sick and dying from the streets and bring comfort and, as far as possible, healing to them – tending their wounds, feeding them, consoling them, at their end being there for them, holding them to her breast as their mother may have done, so they would not be without someone loving them as they drew their last breath. The world would later stand in awe at what she did, but she did not think that way. She understood that what she did was not from her but from God. The Holy Spirit was at work in her, and it was his fruit of generosity, dwelling and working within her, that allowed her to give even when she had nothing else left. The providence of God and his grace, in this fruit, replenished her heart and her soul just as he provided for her work materially.

This booklet is one in a series, *Living Fruitfully*, which explores the fruits of the Holy Spirit – what they are, how they operate in the life of a disciple of Christ, and how the saints show us the way these fruits are manifest and reveal the process of sanctification at work. The fruits are given liberally by God, and among them is the fruit of generosity. Being generous makes us feel good. It is a human thing which reveals that most noble part of our nature. It is also a divine thing: when we are generous we are imitating the One who has been most generous with us. But the dynamic is deeper than that: when we are generous God is present both in the giving and in the receiving. Our generosity has far-reaching consequences, going way beyond that sense of peace or goodwill we feel towards ourselves and others.

St Paul's observation "The Lord loves a cheerful giver" (*2 Co* 9:7) is not simply a beautiful sentiment encouraging Christians to be generous. It reveals a call, an urging, to abandonment, to the very generosity of God; a renouncing of hesitation, begrudging and fearfulness so as to open ourselves up in trust to the mystery of the Spirit working within us, pouring out whatever is within in the service of others, and then, when the store of nature is empty, replenishing it in grace.

The limit of generosity is love, and as God is love, it is eternal and infinite. St Teresa of Calcutta understood that. Though human generosity will eventually come to end, perhaps even when all is given, for those living fruitfully in the Spirit their generosity may have no end since it is immersed in the bounty of the divine. The soul is possessed of an eternal bounty, and in sharing this bounty the soul is sanctified. As grace builds on nature, God transforms this human charity into a divine one. Since charity and generosity are at the very heart of God, those who give themselves to it are taken into the very presence, into the very heart, of God himself.

Generosity as a fruit of the Holy Spirit

The Jewish feast of Pentecost was a harvest festival: a feast of thanksgiving to God for his bounty. That God should choose to send the Holy Spirit on the infant Church on that day was no coincidence: he came to confer his fruitfulness on the Disciples of Christ as a means of beginning the Church's great mission – her being sent out to gather the harvest. The Jewish feast also celebrates the giving of the Torah, the Law of Moses, on Mount Sinai, by which the covenant between God and his chosen people would be established and regulated. Again, it is no coincidence that this anniversary should be chosen: on Pentecost day the Holy Spirit planted his law within the hearts of the disciples as they were sent out into the world with the seed of the new law of the new covenant growing within them to produce a harvest of good works and holiness.

As explained in the first booklet in this *Living Fruitfully* series, on self-control,[1] the fruits of the Holy Spirit are, as the *Catechism of the Catholic Church* defines them, "perfections that the Holy Spirit forms in us as the first fruits of eternal glory".[2] They are given to those who have embraced the Christian life and are seeking to live by the way of virtue in the pursuit of holiness. These twelve fruits seem at first glance to be human actions or attributes, and while initially they are, as grace builds on nature the Holy Spirit transforms them and they come under his control and become supernatural. They are perfected, and with them the person within whom they are working. As a human virtue generosity is noble, but as a fruit by which the Holy Spirit is nourishing and guiding the soul it becomes not only an extraordinary expression of a Christian's selflessness, but the sign of God's bountiful providence and love.

Goodness and generosity

Generosity is the fruit of a transformed heart. It emerges from goodness. Indeed the old translation of the word St Paul uses for this fruit, ἀγαθωσύνη (*agathosune*), was 'goodness'. This word denotes intrinsic goodness and is derived from ἀγαθός (*agathos*), meaning good. It is a biblical and ecclesiastical word, so it is not used in secular Greek. In his Letter to the Galatians, where he lists the fruits of the Spirit, Paul uses it in the context of kindness and beneficence or charity, and from this is derived its translation as 'generosity'. The link between goodness and generosity is established, then, not just in the word but also in the attitude St Paul is asking Christians to have towards others. When it is said, "See how the Christians love each other",[3] that love was to be manifest externally as much as internally, and one of the ways in which this is to be seen is through acts of generosity, be they material or otherwise.

Generosity as a human attribute is simply an act of kindness and goodness to those in need. As a fruit of the Holy Spirit it is concerned not only with the service of those in need, but with the transformation of the soul, through renunciation, to a greater conformity with Christ who was generous in the extreme for the salvation of mankind. Authentic generosity is not mere giving. Generosity, operating as a fruit of the Spirit, is a perfection in which one is called above and beyond the call of duty to be of service to others, be it in a material sense or simply through the gift of our time, our attention, our care. It is a gift of self which is not only selfless, but grounded in love and tied to growth in virtue; as our love becomes purer, so too the nature and extent of our generosity. Ordinarily there is only so much we can do, but extraordinarily, as the Spirit perfects our generosity, we do what we never imagined was possible. Generosity as a fruit excels in renunciation, in death to self and total gift to God and the other. Jesus describes this in his teaching in the Sermon on the Mount, when he says:

> You have heard that it was said, "An eye for an eye and a tooth for a tooth." But I say to you, do not resist one who is evil. But if anyone strikes you on the right cheek, turn to him the other also; and if anyone would sue you and take your coat, let him have your cloak as well; and if anyone forces you to go one mile, go with him two miles. Give to him who begs from you, and do not refuse him who would borrow from you. (*Mt* 5:38-42)

That this teaching on giving is set in the context of giving to enemies and those who hate us is no accident: this is the generosity Christ expects of us. As frail human beings we may well wonder if it is possible, but Christ responds to our doubts simply and concisely: "With men this is impossible, but with God all things are possible" (*Mt* 19:26). It is the Spirit who will not only make this selflessness possible but also turn us into profligates in generosity. It is the Spirit who will help us let go of comfort, and sometimes even need, so we can pour ourselves out in generosity. How is it possible to pour ourselves out? When we are immersed in God and he is our model and our motivation, when we seek to love our neighbour as ourselves, and yes, even our enemies, the charity of Christ within us will teach us how to pour ourselves out. Created as we are in the image and likeness of God, this total gift of self is possible, but only when the fruit of the Spirit has ripened within us and is producing seeds which themselves are beginning to germinate.

Spirit-led generosity

Generosity is a response. On a human level it is a response to those in need; on a spiritual level it is a response to God's generosity to us. In the first, it is an act of charity; in the second it is an act of thanksgiving. Spirit-led generosity is a giving to others and service of others without any hope or expectation of return, and as such, it is a sign of trust in God: as we have given from what we have, God will provide for us. It is an act of faith, an overwhelming confidence in God's bounty that shatters any anxiety we might have and allows us the freedom to give without counting the cost, to serve without any thought for what we lose or what response we might receive.

Generosity involves renunciation, and as a fruit of the Spirit coming to seed within us it becomes a total renunciation for Christ's sake, a forgetfulness of self to embrace the other through love. That complete forgetfulness of self can only emerge after we have abandoned ourselves into the hands and providence of God. This renunciation allows us to become channels for God's grace and his bounty so God can serve his people through us and there is nothing that stands in his way.

When the Spirit takes control of the generous soul he perfects that generosity, turning a human response into the action of God working in and through that person. The soul now participates in the work of God as he pours out his goodness, his bounty and his help to others. Jesus reveals this in his teaching on judging others, in which he urges generosity. But God himself provides for the generous giver. The more you give the more you receive and so the more you can give again: the Spirit becomes the one who directs the alms from his own store.

The prophet Malachi is given a similar insight into this provision of the Spirit when he writes this prophecy: "Bring the full tithes into the storehouse, that there may be food in my house; and thereby put me to the test, says the Lord of hosts, if I will not open the windows of heaven for you and pour down for you an overflowing blessing" (*Ml* 3:10). In this, God seems to be daring his people to be generous, to test him: whatever they give into his house he will not only return, but will do so in abundance – he himself will make provision from his own storehouse. The saints have often dared God to provide for them when they have turned to the poor with empty hands. God loves this challenge and he will not be found wanting. He may well be creative in the way he provides, surprising us; but he will not fail.

Generosity in God

That God urges generosity in his people should come as no surprise when we look to the Holy Trinity and catch a glimpse of his inner life. Generosity is inherent in God: it is central to the life of the three Persons of the Trinity. In exploring that inner life, in as far as it can be known, theologians down the centuries have identified a dynamic which is referred to as *perichoresis* (περιχώρησις). This Greek term, first used by early Church thinkers in the context of the relationship between Christ's divine and human natures, is first employed in a Trinitarian context by St Maximus the Confessor. *Perichoresis* is derived from two Greek words: *peri* (περι) meaning 'around', and the verb *chorein* (χώρηιν) meaning to make room for, to go into and to take hold. The Latin translation of the term, *circumincessio*, led to an understanding of it referring to a divine dance – a movement around and within. The term in its theological sense refers to the indwelling of the Persons of the Holy Trinity with each other, a total giving of each Person to the others in the most intimate way. This concept of *perichoresis* reveals the nature of true love in the heart of the Trinity: it is one of total gift, utter generosity.

In his theology, St Gregory Nazianzen used the term *perichoresis* to explore the two natures of Christ, understanding the term to include "flowing into one another, according to the law of their intimate union".[4] St John Damascene in his writings developed it as a means of understanding the inner life of the Trinity and resolving problems regarding the exact identity of God as One and as three Persons. Theologians reflecting on the concept saw that it did indeed reveal an important dimension of the inner life of God. Translating St Gregory's understanding of the term to explore the life of the Trinity, it was revealed that the three Persons' mutual indwelling was a pouring of each Person into the others in love and total gift, this occurring eternally within the Godhead. It is in this context that we understand that the Son is eternally begotten of the Father and that the Holy Spirit proceeds eternally from the Father and the Son. Each Person of the Trinity gives all to the others in an act of eternal and divine generosity that is true love. This is what St John means when he says that God *is* love. The Latin term of *circumincessio*, implying a dance, is not too far off the mark as the movement of this pouring out of the divine Persons is like a great dance: a moving in and through the others, what we can understand to be a living for each other.

To become more like him

This extraordinary revelation of the life of God reveals the divine source of generosity. God is, by his eternal nature, generous, because in the heart of his divine life is giving. God urges generosity among his adopted children so we can become more like him. As God is generous within, that generosity cannot remain within, but it pours out from the three Persons and their union; and so God creates and permeates his creation with his generosity.

The scriptures bear witness to this generosity from the first verses of the Book of Genesis as he creates; but the creation of the world was not the first expression of God's generosity. The creation of the world and the creation of men and women is the manner in which we are first acquainted directly with the generosity of God. As the chaos was transformed into the universe, God the great artist brought into being a most marvellous work: complex, beautiful and rich, a world not only to sustain life but to offer meaning and intrigue. God the creator did not mean only to make but to bring joy. When the Holy Spirit breathed over the face of the abyss (see *Gn* 1:2), he not only brought life but he generously poured out the imagination and adventure of God so making what was nothing rich and exciting.

When he breathed life into Adam, God did not hold back either: he made man and woman in his own image and likeness. This most daring, and perhaps some with common sense might say, foolhardy action, brought into existence beings that would seek to be like God because they were intended from the beginning to be like God, to share his eternal life. This creature resembled God in what was given, in what is part of our human nature. The generosity of God flowed out as he heaped intelligence, ability, creativity, sensitivity, wit, immortality and free will on this being. Great risks were indeed taken, but God wanted to give all; and though he knew how things would turn out in the short term, he also knew how things would turn out in the long term, so it was worth it. This creature, the union of flesh and spirit, was destined to be holy, to share in the very holiness of God. This earthly life was a transitional stage where men and women would prove their mettle and advance in virtue to holiness and the life that was its eternal reward. Even in this creation the interior generosity of God is manifest: the Father created it all in, with and for the Son, and the Spirit vivified it all with his presence, moving across the abyss and the chaos to order it and mould it according to the will of the Father. And when the Father gazed on Adam, the first human being, he saw the face of his own beloved Son, the Second Person of the Trinity, when he would be made man as part of God's plan for the salvation he knew would be necessary. God's extraordinary generosity looked even then beyond the disaster which was coming.

An unworthy race?

God's generosity found a new outlet as he nurtured an often rebellious mankind, conferring his grace and help and revealing himself even when mankind proved ungrateful or uninterested, though some responded in kind: Abel and the mysterious Enoch who "walked with God" and was taken up into heaven (see *Gn* 5:24). In choosing one man, and from him a small tribe as his chosen people, God was not only carrying out his plan of salvation and preparing redemption, he was also seeking out a family on which to confer his gifts and graces to raise them up. He chose the weakest of all, not only to demonstrate his power but to reveal that in his generosity he seeks out the smallest, the most miserable. God is not interested in prestige; rather he seeks to better the plight of the poor and raise up those most affected by the weakness of our human nature.

The children of Abraham seemed to have little going for them. In the eyes of the world, these Hebrews, later Jews, were despised and mocked – an unworthy race in the minds of the strong, yet they were the ones who received the greatest portion of God's love and mercy. Though they fell, and made stupid decisions and silly alliances; though they were often unfaithful and ungrateful; though they were at times as cold as ice or driven to irrational extremes, God looked on them with the intensity of his generous love, made a covenant with them and called them his people. In the fullness of time when the Second Person of the Trinity descended to become man to win the salvation of the world, he became one of them. The Jewish people are certainly the living embodiment of the utter faithfulness and generosity of God.

The Incarnation and the Paschal Mystery are the greatest outpourings of the generosity of God. In these mysteries we see the interior dynamic of the Trinity as the Son in his love says yes to the Father's will; we see the Father's love for and generosity to the world in the way that, as St John notes, "God so loved the world that he gave his only Son" to be a sacrifice to redeem us (*Jn* 3:16). In the Incarnation the Son stripped himself of his glory and became man.

This extraordinary mystery reveals the outpouring of the Son in the inner life of the Holy Trinity. In his living among us, Christ brought the life of God into our midst, the miracles and teachings revealing the presence of the healing and wisdom of God. The Lord's pity towards the sick and sinners is to be noted above all: God continues to reach out to the weakest and most miserable to raise them up. Christ's public ministry is a testament to generosity. He did not spare himself, but preached the Word and healed the sick, refusing none of them; he forgave sinners, even the most notorious, and offered them a new life. He did not come to the healthy, but to the sick who needed a doctor, a divine physician (cf. *Lk* 5:31-32). Going beyond the realm of Judaism he preached in pagan territory, in the Decapolis, revealing that God was now reaching out to restore all humanity.

Emptying of self in love

The depths of God's generosity are seen in the offering, Passion and death of Jesus. God himself provided the sacrifice to redeem mankind (cf. *Gn* 22:7-8), and the victim was himself: the Son of God made man. We must remember, however, that this offering was a difficult one. As St Paul notes in his Letter to the Romans, it is hard to die, and though one might be prepared to die for a good person "God shows his love for us in that while we were yet sinners Christ died for us" (*Rm* 5:7). Jesus struggled in his humanity with this offering of himself; his agony in the garden reveals the dynamic of the hypostatic union as the human will of Jesus is brought into complete harmony with his divine will and his loving generosity unto death.

The great symbol of God's generosity is the image of the dead Christ on the cross. In his desolation, those words from the cross, "My God, my God, why have you forsaken me?" (*Mt* 27:46) do not just reveal the extent of his suffering, but the nature and extent of his offering: an oblation revealing the inner life of the Trinity, the *perichoresis*, now a drama taking place on the cross. Jesus' dying on the cross is a revelation of God – his salvific work, his inner life: the mystery of God is laid bare in those dreadful moments as Christ gasps for his last breath. That last breath is Christ's complete emptying of self in love. Christ naked, abused, tortured, worn-out, dead, and yet there was more to come: the Incarnate Son of God still gives. With the piercing of his heart, Jesus yields his last drop of blood and the last drop of water – it is not over until all is given, poured out and offered as an oblation.

The gift of the Eucharist

But God was not finished; he continues to give, and one of his greatest gifts is the Eucharist. In this sacrament we are given Christ himself, for in receiving him, we are drawn into the life of God, where Christ pours out graces upon us and shares with us the intimacy of his inner life. In the Eucharist he fulfils his promise to remain with us until the end of time. As we eat his Body, his life sustains and heals ours; and in his presence in our churches and chapels he silently and generously makes himself available for us at every hour of the day and night. There in the tabernacle the Lord waits upon us as a servant at a banquet (*Lk* 12:37), but he also seeks to inspire and to teach. Christ poured out as a libation, the gift of a generous God, now means to teach his disciples to do the same, for it is only in this that they will come to be like God. Adam and Eve's mistake was to think they could become like God by taking what was not theirs for themselves (*Gn* 3:4-7); in fact the opposite is true: it is in giving, and giving all, that we are divinised.

God's original plan to divinise us is still in place. It is not negated or abandoned, not destroyed by our sin, but enhanced because now in his generosity he shows mercy; as St Paul explains, "For God has consigned all men to disobedience, that he may have mercy upon all" (*Rm* 11:32). Mercy is the greatest expression of God's generosity towards us; indeed, as St John Paul II tells us in his encyclical *Dives in Misericordia*, it is his greatest attribute.[5] That God created us reveals his generosity in generating life and sustaining it; that

God saved us when we fell and restored us in mercy reveals the infinite depths of that generosity – that it is truly the crown of his goodness and love.

Material generosity

Following his encounter with Jesus, Zacchaeus, now a man converted, revealed the effects of his conversion by making restitution for his financial sins, not merely paying back what he owed, but giving more in reparation – an act of generosity that reveals the authenticity of his conversion (see *Lk* 19:1-10). Generosity as a response to the presence and work of Christ is not unusual; it is always the sign of true faith and the presence of the Spirit. The heart immersed in the action of God imitates God by the desire to give; this is at first as a human response, but as the Spirit prompts and guides, it becomes a giving to the point where natural resources give way to providence. Human beings, made in the image and likeness of God, find it most natural to be generous. Miserliness is a subhuman, even an anti-human, state of mind and being; its effect is the shrivelling of the heart and soul of the miser. Charles Dickens in one of his most famous books, *A Christmas Carol*, presents his protagonist Ebenezer Scrooge as a withered and lifeless old man; it is his conversion to the spirit of generosity which revives him, and while not lifting the number of years from his head, it makes him youthful and joyful. Human beings come to life when they are generous; this is why it seems so good to give, why one feels happy and noble: it is the most natural thing in the world. As grace builds on nature, this human generosity, when led through the work of the Spirit to his fruit of generosity, becomes something truly extraordinary and marvellous, not just changing the heart and soul from tardiness and selfishness to levity and joy, but transforming the entire person in sanctity.

Mankind's dependence on God

From the beginning, God urged material generosity on his people to aid their transformation to a people civilised by the covenant. In the Law given to Moses God commanded that his chosen people should care for the poor – for the orphaned and the widowed and the stranger (*Dt* 24:21). His command to reap the harvest in the vineyard, olive grove or field only once was intended to leave food for the poor who would come to glean. God reminded them that they were once slaves – they had been oppressed, they knew the sting of hunger and the reality of an uncertain future. Now that they had a livelihood, each was to give in accordance with what they had received (*Dt* 16:17). They were not to take advantage of the poor, and even if the poor had to repay a debt, if necessary that repayment was to be renounced and returned to ensure people had food to eat and a cloak to cover them at night (see *Dt* 24:12). God's establishing the year of jubilee was the means of restoring a livelihood to the poor, freeing them from a servitude their poverty demanded. This year was to remind the chosen ones to give freely, without any begrudging, and in doing so receive the Lord's blessing (see *Dt* 15). The Israelites heeded God's command, for the most part. We see an example of this in the story of Ruth as she and her mother-in-law come to the fields of Boaz to glean what was left (*Rt* 2:23). The goodness of Boaz is seen in his adherence to this law of charity. However, others were not so observant and so earned the wrath of the prophets for their neglect of the poor. These prophets, Amos foremost among them, condemned those who reserved their wealth for themselves and forgot the poor at their gates, or oppressed the poor and needy for their own enrichment.

Such was the command to charity that God enshrined the requirement of generosity not just in the Law but in the very fabric of the daily life of Israel. While God promises the tribes an inheritance in the Promised

Land in accordance with his revelations to Abraham and Moses, the tribe of Levi does not receive land, they will "have no portion or inheritance with Israel", rather "they shall eat the offerings by fire to the Lord, and his rightful dues" (*Dt* 18:1-8). It falls to the others to provide the inheritance of the Levites through their offerings to God and through their generosity. This is, of course, a symbol of all mankind's dependence on God: he is the only inheritance we have. This decision of God's places responsibility on the Israelites to look out from themselves to others who now have a claim on them for their livelihood. There is no place for selfishness in the covenant; as God has given, so too those in the communion of love with him must give. Generosity is not subject to a whim or noble gesture or even to a surplus: it is a duty established in the context of the Law of God.

Treasure in heaven

The Jews understood that those who were faithful to this law of charity, who were generous above and beyond the call of duty, would receive the Lord's abundant blessing. The story of Elijah and the widow reveals this most clearly (*1 K* 17:8-18:24). Arriving at the home of a starving woman and her son during the great drought called down upon the Northern Kingdom of Israel (Samaria) for its infidelity, Elijah asks for food, and though she has little, the widow agrees to include him in what she thinks will be her last meal: she cannot turn away the hungry. Even with the little that is left, she shares with another who is hungry. Her generosity is repaid by the continual replenishing of her supplies by miraculous means and later by the greater miracle of her son being restored to life when he suddenly dies. The Jewish people cherished such stories, which informed their own tradition of hospitality and charity.

The gospels continued to urge the faithful to embrace this generosity. The widow who gave from "all the living that she had" (*Lk* 21:4), for example, not only received the Lord's praise in the gospel, but she serves as the example of generosity for the Disciples of Christ. Jesus reiterates this sacrificial gift in his encounter with the rich young man as recorded in St Matthew's Gospel (*Mt* 19:16-26). This unnamed individual seeks perfection; he has followed all the commandments with great fidelity and generosity, but Jesus tells him that if he seeks perfection there is still one thing he lacks: "go and sell what you own and give the money to the poor,… then and come, follow me". The young man cannot do this and he walks away sad, but the Lord urges those who follow him to embrace this generosity as a means not only of helping the poor, but of dying to self and being born to holiness: generosity clears space within the self to allow the Spirit of God to take up his home in us. It is through sacrifice that natural generosity can give way to that generosity which is the fruit of the Spirit.

Jesus is keen to stress that this personal renunciation is not ignored by God, rather it is the means to attaining a greater treasure in heaven. As the rich young man walks away downcast, the apostles are shocked: who can be saved? They have given up everything to follow him; what will they have? For their sacrifice, Jesus tells them, they will receive a hundredfold back and inherit eternal life. This promise for those who are generous beyond what seem like natural limits is reinforced by the Lord in his parables. The man who sells all to buy a field finds a treasure (*Mt* 13:44), the merchant who finds the pearl of great price sells all his valuables to get it (*Mt* 13:45); these men had to take a risk and sacrifice all to afford the treasure they found. So too with generosity: the disciples who risk all will not be forgotten; they too will find a treasure and that treasure is the Kingdom of God; it is already in their midst (cf. *Lk* 17:21) and, as heirs, it will be theirs for eternity (cf. *Lk* 22:29-30).

Corporal works of mercy

Embracing the risk of generosity allows the Spirit to strengthen the soul with his fruits. Until he had given up all he had, St Anthony of Egypt, for example, was not free to go out into the mysterious life of the desert where he encountered God. As St Athanasius records in his biography of the father of monasticism, Anthony, having heard the story of the rich young man, gave up most of his possessions, but still held some back. It was the gospel again which prompted him to let go of the last of his wealth so he could be truly free to follow his call. All the saints took this risk to reach out and assist the poor. The Spirit urged them away from catering for their own needs to meeting the needs of others.

The Church as Mother, seeking to inspire her children to embrace this way of generosity, encourages them to carry out particular merciful acts, what are usually called the seven corporal works of mercy. These corporal works serve two purposes: the first and most obvious is the provision of care and services for those in need; but secondly they are the "training wheels" to get Christians off to a good start and prepare the ground within them for the Spirit to work. Leading them to a greater engagement with himself through these charitable works, the Spirit, having planted the seed of generosity within, nurtures its growth into the tree which bears the fruit to nourish the soul in the way of renunciation for Christ's sake. These corporal works of mercy are:

To feed the hungry;
To give drink to the thirsty;
To clothe the naked;
To shelter the homeless;
To visit the sick;
To visit prisoners and ransom those in captivity;
To bury the dead.

These works are simple and obvious, and sometimes challenging. They provide a framework for the faithful to respond to God's call to love our neighbour. The Catholic Church is the largest charity in the world and in history, not because she is a two thousand year old universal institution, but because thousands upon thousands of her members, down the centuries and today, realised that they were loved by God, and in response to the generosity of his love, sought to be generous themselves. Often simply responding to needs they saw in front of them, they took the corporal works of mercy as the charter for their activities and they reached out.

The act of generosity

The most vital of these works is providing the most basic needs to the poor and this has been at the forefront in the charitable work of Christians, a service given to all regardless of who they are or what they do, or what they have done. This act of generosity sees only need and responds to it. One modern example of this material generosity is Blessed Ceferino Jiménez Malla, the "Gypsy Saint". One of the martyrs of the Spanish Civil War, he was condemned to death for refusing to renounce his rosary beads and was shot, with his bishop, on 9th August 1936. Born into a Catholic Romani family, he did not pay much attention to his faith; even when he married his wife, Teresa, he was not bothered to solemnise the marriage before God, preferring a traditional Roma ceremony. Cattle traders, and quite wealthy, he and Teresa had no children of their own, but in 1909 they adopted his niece, Pepita. Following a major conversion Ceferino discovered Christ; he and Teresa regularised their marriage in 1912 and began to live an intense Christian life.

When Teresa died in 1922, Ceferino was free to devote himself in a more intense way to the needs of others. He trained as a catechist and taught the faith to local children. Though he had always been generous, often helping out members of his family and other Roma who were in need, he felt a call to a deeper generosity. He joined the Society of St Vincent de Paul, and then, on a personal level, he began to distribute his wealth. Numerous stories tell of his extraordinary generosity. When his daughter

Pepita was married and comfortable, Ceferino, now a Franciscan tertiary, sought to give to the point of utter poverty. Living a life bordering on destitution, he gave whatever he received to the poor and needy, seeking out the destitute and preferring to go hungry rather than see another deprived. Far from feeling the pinch, Ceferino found true happiness and consolation as a servant of the generosity of God. His martyrdom crowned this life of charity.

Ecce Homo

Some saints, not content with individual works of charity, sought to found great charitable organisations to care for the poor and the sick in a more efficient and organised way – their generosity was destined by God to last long beyond their lives. Among these is one of the Church's great servants of the homeless, St Albert Chmielowski, a Polish painter and former soldier. He knew the ravages of war and isolation. Injured in battle, he lost a leg, but also lost his faith in God and man. When he was finally converted to Christ, he realised he needed to reach out to others who faced desolation in their lives, and then heard the call to serve the homeless poor in Kraków, of which they were many. Old and young, ill in body and mind, many addicted to alcohol, often despairing, these poor men and women had nowhere to go, many of them perishing in the freezing Polish winters. Albert saw the suffering Christ in them. He had once painted an image of the *Ecce Homo*, Christ crowned with thorns, scourged, mocked and now exposed to the mockery of the world: he saw this Christ in those lying in the streets – they too were exposed to the hardship and neglect of the world. His heart was torn apart with pity and bound back again with zeal. Professing vows as a Third Order Franciscan, Albert left everything, took up residence in a homeless shelter, and there put his life at the service of those in the homeless shelters and on the streets. Knowing that this problem was not of his time only, in 1888 he founded congregations of brothers and sisters to ensure that when he died, his mission of mercy would not die with him – the homeless poor would have homes and servants in his spiritual sons and daughters.

Another founder, St Joseph Benedict Cottolengo, is worthy of particular mention; he founded the Little House of Divine Providence in Turin in 1828. The title is deceptive – it is not little, but now a great institution that cares for numerous sick and poor. During his lifetime, St Joseph Benedict trusted God's providence to provide for his needs – the fruit of generosity had, in time, long surpassed the natural urge with a supernatural expectation in God's bounty. So much did he trust that, each night, whatever money he had left over he bagged and threw out of his bedroom window into the street for whatever poor person would find it, confident that God would provide whatever was needed for the next day. Each morning he woke to a benefactor arriving to help the good father and his pious works. It is interesting to note that the Little House of Divine Providence stood next door to St John Bosco's home for young boys and girls, a charity always in need of funds. It did not take Don Bosco long to learn of his holy neighbour's nightly custom and so it was usually him standing in the street waiting to catch the bag of money when it came flying out of Cottolengo's window.

A divine gift

The fruit of the Spirit does more than transform human generosity into a divine gift; it also confers virtues to help the soul in the administration of this generosity. Two of these are worth noting. First, it counsels prudence. The Lord loves a cheerful giver, but he is not impressed if the giver starves his family to feed the poor. The first act of generosity is to one's own – we cannot deprive those dependent on us of their basic needs to provide for the needs of others. Generosity which is authentically the fruit of the Spirit is also the fruit of wisdom. It must of course teach our dependents the way of sacrifice and generosity, but it never forces it upon them. The man or woman who lets their children go hungry so they can feed the poor is not operating according to the Spirit. That said, the saints have also become teachers to their children in the way of generosity, reminding all of us that as we seek to allow this fruit to take control of our lives, the fruit of generosity, like all the fruits of the Spirit, is to be evangelical in a missionary sense.

Second the fruit of the Spirit serves an important role in fortifying the soul against despair. When one responds to the call of the needy, and seeks to fulfil the requirements of charity, there is the danger of being overwhelmed by constant demands and the sheer extent of poverty in the world. Too often heroic souls have shrivelled up under the weight of need; many have lost faith and become cynical and hardened. When the Spirit takes possession of the soul and nurtures his harvest within, the fruit sustains and feeds the soul to strengthen it and console it. It confers hope and patience, peace and zeal, but it also counsels wisdom, reminding the person that they do what they can do with what they have and with what God has chosen to provide, and then leave the rest to God and others. Jesus did say that the poor will always be with us (*Mt* 26:11), and this must temper zeal: we alone cannot meet every need.

The saints, as they worked hard and gave up their lives in the service of the poor, were tutored by this wisdom. They never despaired, but trusted in God – his providence gave what was needed for what they had to do. This wisdom can be seen in St Teresa of Calcutta. As she left her convent, she could have been overwhelmed by what awaited her on the streets. All she could do at the start, realistically, was to pick up the first dying man she saw and care for him. Then, perhaps a second and a third, maybe a fourth; when her followers came, more could be taken in. God would provide for that, and in time she found he did.

The gift of self

At the beginning of the twentieth century, during a night of adoration, a young Italian man, gazing at the Blessed Sacrament in the monstrance, made a promise. He felt a sense of obligation "to do something for God and the men of the new century".[6] This young man was a seminarian, James Alberione, and understanding that he was obliged to serve the Church, he offered himself and his entire life to the service of God. That generosity, a movement of the Holy Spirit within him, was a response in faith to "a particular light" that emanated from the Host in the monstrance. James would offer seventy years, years of priestly service and dedication to God and the Church, founding no less than ten religious congregations and forming the Pauline Family.

Blessed James Alberione's offering was one which revealed generosity as a fruit of the Spirit, a deep divesting of self in order to give oneself completely to the will and service of God. Generosity in material terms is indeed noble, and when it emerges from reliance on the providence of God, it can be miraculous. However, it gives way to that generosity which marks the gift of self which is a more fundamental, much more personal offering, leading a person from the comfort of putting their wealth and material possessions on the line, to giving their time, their lives, even their destiny. This generosity is an oblation, one which requires resolve and death to self – reaching out to others in service, giving time and effort. In a radical way, it finds its most potent expression in embracing the consecrated life in its various forms where one is led in a direction that might not have been chosen initially (cf. *Jn* 21:18). The Lord puts it succinctly when he says, "Greater love has no man than this, that a man lay down his life for his friends" (*Jn* 15:13) – generosity of self is the greater love, and the extent of that love depends on and is revealed by how much is given.

For Christians material generosity should lead to the gift of self, the two are intertwined. The total gift of self is difficult, most especially when the fruit of the Spirit has not fully ripened within the soul. There can be a tremendous struggle as what is lost is measured up against what is gained and as the Spirit tries to divest the soul of weights and measures to see only love and necessity. St Paul acknowledges this, for example when he writes to the Romans telling them that it can be difficult for one to die even for a good person (cf. *Rm* 5:7); though Paul is speaking of the Lord dying for the ungodly, we can also understand that making a sacrifice for others can be difficult if that sacrifice requires our death, be it physical death or, in the context of this reflection, a death to self. The most basic and primeval instinct is self-preservation at all costs and this conflicts with the most Godlike in generosity.

A life of service

This struggle can be seen even in saints, where the fruit of the Spirit often had to ripen under great duress and pain. St Gabriel Possenti offers one such example. Also known as St Gabriel of Our Lady of Sorrows, he is now venerated as one of the great young saints of the Church. Gabriel struggled and fought with his vocation. He was very much the young man about town: gregarious, fond of the ladies, liking his drink, as God was calling he was resisting. He fell seriously ill twice – the wakeup call – and each time he promised God that he would enter religious life if he were healed. He was healed, but he reneged on his promise. More disasters befell him and each time he saw the hand of God beckoning him to offer his life in service; and though he grew more devout, he still resisted. He at last relented and entered the Passionists in 1856, the fruit of generosity having finally ripened within him – though just about: he had asked a girl to marry him and was waiting for her answer when he surrendered to God.

St Gabriel went on to live an intense, if short, religious life, leaving a reputation of total generosity to the will of God and of service to his brothers in the Congregation. A similar struggle can be seen in another who was called to an extraordinary life of service to the Church: St Faustina Kowalska. Now venerated as the apostle or secretary of Divine Mercy (as Jesus himself called her), her own journey to the consecrated life was as hesitant as Gabriel's. She too resisted, though she was already experiencing mystical phenomenon. The Lord had to appear to her on a dance floor and opine, "How long shall I put up with you and how long will you keep putting me off?" to bring her to her senses.[7] Again, the fruit of generosity had to ripen, and it did at that moment. Faustina began a long, hard pilgrimage to the convent where her resolve to enter was tested many times, but there can be little doubt, given her serene persistence, that the Spirit was moving within her and nurturing her resolve. Once the soul responds, grace can abound. The person is stretched, sometimes, it seems, beyond their ability, but as with all learning curves, it is necessary for growth – the fruit of generosity confers certain elasticity.

Though not yet a saint (the Cause for his beatification is now, rightly, being considered), the hero of the Titanic, Fr Thomas Byles, reveals the fruit of generosity at work, with the Spirit solidifying it with tremendous courage. A convert to Catholicism, in 1912 serving as a priest in St Helen's Parish, Chipping Ongar in Essex, he was travelling on the Titanic to the United States to officiate at his brother's wedding. Fr Byles spent his last hours preparing the anguished on the sinking ship for death: hearing their confessions for as long as he could, then administering General Absolution and leading those who clung to him for comfort in prayer. Twice he was offered a place in the lifeboats but he refused: his place, his priestly heart told him, was with those who would perish in the waters. He literally laid down his life to be of service to those who were in need in extreme and fatal circumstances. In those fearful and horrific moments, the Holy Spirit took possession of his servant and helped him put generosity before self-preservation.

Simple in holiness

Another who manifested the same generosity unto death was the Venerable Edel Quinn, Envoy of the Legion of Mary. A quiet and simple soul in her holiness, Edel joined the Legion in Dublin in 1927 as a means of serving Our Lady. Her life to this point had been plagued by tuberculosis (TB); she had spent eighteen months in a sanatorium prior to joining the Legion, but the disease had left its mark on her health. Despite this she offered herself as Envoy to spread the Legion in East Africa. The founder of the Legion, the Servant of God Frank Duff, though at first hesitant, saw that God was at work in her: her generosity was not the expression of human optimism and desire, but rather the Spirit setting her on fire to bring this Marian work to the missionary Church. He accepted her offer and though he had a battle on his hands to get the Legion's central council, Concilium, to agree, he managed to have her appointed. Arriving in Mombasa in 1936, Edel soared like a fire throughout East and Central Africa founding numerous praesidia until her death in 1944. TB gradually claimed her life, but it was no match for her determination. Though she knew she would die, and that staying in Ireland would have perhaps allowed her many years of life, her graced generosity led her to sacrifice that in order to serve Our Lady and the mission given to the Legion to work for Christ. Though shocked when news of her death reached them, the members of the Legion in Ireland realised that gentle, quiet, frail Edel was sustained by a power greater than that possessed by any mere mortal. Her life was a miracle, and it was so because she had abandoned herself to the work of the Spirit within her, and the fruit of generosity gave her strength of will and body to help her achieve what God had called her to do.

Edel's example is actually at the heart of the theology and work of the Legion of Mary, which is the living out of the Act of Total Consecration to Christ through Our Lady as taught and promoted by St Louis Marie de Montfort in his *Treatise on True Devotion to the Blessed Virgin Mary*. Often dismissed by the religiously sophisticated as too pious and too extreme, this spirituality is one in which the movement of the Spirit is all too obvious, since it leads the one making the Consecration to a complete abandonment in an act that has the hallmarks of holy profligacy. In this Consecration, the soul is invited to utter abandonment into the hands of Mary so she can lead the soul to Christ, and guide the soul in faithful and heroic work for Christ and the Church. It is an inspired generosity that leads the soul to make this offering. St Louis Marie uses the concept of slavery to reveal the nature of this act of self-giving, even urging devotees to wear a little chain as the symbol and reminder of their offering.

Inspired by the Spirit

One extraordinary example of this utter gift of self to the point of slavery is that offered by St John of Matha and St Felix of Valois, the founders of the Trinitarian

Order. St John was a French priest, given to charitable works since his youth, who was deeply distressed by the plight of Christians taken into slavery. On 28th January 1193, having celebrated his First Mass after ordination, he had a vision of Christ holding by the hands two captives in chains. One of these two held a staff with a blue and white cross. John went into a period of solitude to discern what the Lord intended him to do in response to this vision. During this time he met a holy hermit, Felix of Valois, and together they prayed and discerned. A further vision of the blue and white cross in the antlers of a stag convinced them both that they were to found an Order to help and relieve slaves. They founded the Trinitarians and received approval from Pope Innocent III in 1198. However, the Spirit inspired them to add a fourth vow for the members of the Order – that if necessary to free a slave, the Trinitarian was to take that slave's place.

St John spent the rest of his life travelling Europe and North Africa, bringing relief to slaves, raising money to liberate them and frequenting slave markets to attempt to secure the release of those on sale. A number of members, in accordance with their vow and immersed in the fruit of generosity, took the place of slaves. But there was another who had to make a radical offering, though often forgotten. While St John lived an adventurous life, his co-founder, St Felix, was chained to the desk of bureaucracy and organisation. It fell to him to establish the Order and to run it, carrying out the daily martyrdom of drudgery. He became a slave himself to serve the vision and those who were on the mission fields. Often the fruit of generosity ripens and spreads its new seeds in the hidden places, where few see the heroism and sacrifice, in a life as dry as dust.

On fire with the Spirit

One of the modern Church's outstanding saints with regard to the fruit of generosity is St Damien of Moloka'i. Born in Belgium, Damien is more associated with Hawai'i, usually seen as a tropical paradise, but whose stunning landscape and lush vegetation hid terrible secrets and inhuman suffering: leprosy was raging among the native peoples. Believing the disease to be highly contagious, and terrified of an epidemic, the authorities established a leper colony on the remote Kalaupapa peninsula on the island of Moloka'i. Separated from the rest of the island by cliffs and surrounded by treacherous sea currents, the peninsula was a natural fortress, a prison for the sick and dying. In reality it became a hellhole. Deeply concerned for the souls of those abandoned to die on the peninsula, the Catholic bishop of Honolulu, Bishop Louis Désiré Maigret, issued an invitation for priests to consider volunteering to spend three months ministering to the sick and dying there. Among the volunteers was Damien who volunteered to be the first. As he left for his three months, the bishop warned him not to touch the lepers, otherwise he might catch the disease and have to stay. In reality this was what Damien intended – with generosity of heart, the young priest was going to sacrifice his life for the lepers.

Damien embraced the lepers, not just physically, but spiritually and emotionally: he was their father. He gave of himself without measure. He believed all things were possible – the fruit of generosity had planted in him an eternal hope and the tenacity to ensure that hope was fulfilled. He administered the sacraments and formed souls, but he also cared for the lepers, tended their sores, fed them and made them as comfortable as he could. He prepared them to die; and when they died he made their coffins and buried them. He built them proper homes, an infirmary, and an orphanage for the children. There were many children thrown onto the island to fend for themselves; Damien took them under his wing and helped them live out as well as they could whatever life was left to them.

Damien spared nothing for his children, and was tenacious in demands for more money, more resources, more food and more volunteers, but his tenacity often infuriated his superiors. While the bishop who originally sent him to Moloka'i, Bishop Maigret, was determined to get Damien whatever he needed, his successor, Bishop Hermann Koeckemann, was not as indulgent. He and Damien's religious superior, Fr Léonor Fouesnel, were often frustrated by Damien's constant demands, usually delivered in his rough and peasant way. They were not bad men, indeed both did a great deal of good for poor Catholics in Hawai'i, but they too were encountering an immovable and awkward force: a saint on fire with the Spirit and extraordinary generosity who expected an endless bounty and was determined to get it. They failed to see that Damien's insistence was not just stubbornness, but the Spirit speaking through him and pushing them to the limits of generosity.

This is a point to be noted for those growing in the fruits of the Spirit: when the fruit of generosity has taken possession of a soul and is nourishing it to produce a bountiful harvest among those served, this can create difficulties in others who are not as advanced in or privy to the workings of grace in a particular context. These servants of the Spirit will be misunderstood, even by people in the Church, even by Church officials who know the theology of the Spirit but can at times fail to see it at work around them. But in such cases, the fruit also serves to feed and sustain the soul in grace as it continues its work in difficult situations, and such was the case with St Damien. He was frustrated by his superiors, at times overwhelmed by the situation of his lepers, and angry at the tardiness and bureaucracy of the government and Church to meet their needs. Did he go too far? At times, yes; but the lepers, his children, had the first claim on his heart and he cannot be faulted for constantly thinking about them and working out what he needed to get for them. It was a father's love and the zeal which the fruit of the Spirit nurtured in him.

Forgiveness

One dimension of the generosity of the gift of self which may not be first in our thoughts is that of forgiveness. As discussed earlier, mercy is the expression of God's generosity to us; and so too with us: forgiveness is the most pure fruit of generosity, and as we acknowledge with great humility God's generosity to us, we are urged to give the alms of mercy to others. Indeed we are urged to this generosity in the very prayer Jesus gave us, the "Our Father", where we pray (perhaps unconsciously at times) "Forgive us our trespasses *AS* we forgive those who trespass against us". If we are mean-spirited with others, then God will be likewise with us, but if we are generous in mercy, then God will be so with us; as Jesus explicitly tells us: "if you do not forgive others, your Father will not forgive your failings either" (*Mt* 6:15).

This generosity is potently seen in two events concerning the life and death of St Maria Goretti. As is well known, Maria was attacked by a young man, Alessandro Serenelli, whose respect and sensibilities for others was worn away by a lust fed by his addiction to pornography. Maria, the object of his desires, had rejected his advances, but on 5th July 1902, armed with a knife, he tried to force her to yield. When she refusing him, he stabbed her over forty times. Before she died the next day Maria forgave him with all her heart, praying that he would be in heaven with her. She was true to her act of forgiveness: though Alessandro refused to acknowledge his guilt and festered with bitterness in prison, Maria did not give up on him. As he later related, in 1908 she appeared to him in a dream and urged him to accept her forgiveness and repent. He finally broke down and embraced his victim's generosity.

The second incident followed many years later. Having spent twenty-seven years in prison, Alessandro was released in 1929. It seems it took him five years to work up the courage to do what he needed to do: ask pardon of Maria's mother, Assunta. Life had been hard for Assunta. Her husband died while she was still a young woman and she had to raise her children in dreadful conditions; then the murder of her saintly daughter was a sorrow which broke her heart, as any parent can imagine. On Christmas Eve 1934, as she was preparing to go to Midnight Mass, Alessandro turned up at her door. On his knees and in tears he begged her forgiveness. It became obvious that Maria Goretti's holiness was not plucked from the ground: she was well tutored at her mother's knee. Assunta embraced Alessandro saying "How can I refuse to forgive you when Maria did?" Later that night, the two attended Midnight Mass and received Holy Communion side by side at the altar. Assunta adopted Alessandro as a member of her family. As he lived the rest of his life as a gardener in a Capuchin friary, he was known to often say "Maria's forgiveness saved me." Given the circumstances and suffering for both daughter and mother, this wholehearted generosity of forgiveness was surely the fruit of the Spirit working in them: to forget self and think of the other – in this case, another's salvation. As this was the motivation for Maria and Assunta, so it was also for James Alberione, John of Matha, Damien of Moloka'i and countless other holy men and women who understood that the greatest gift they could give God and their neighbour was the gift of self: to lay down their lives for their friends – there is no greater love than that.[8]

Martyrdom

As the Lord's teaching, "A man can have no greater love than to lay down his life for his friend" (*Jn* 15:13), is one of complete self-gift, one immersed in the fruit of generosity, its highest expression is martyrdom. It may seem strange to equate martyrdom with generosity as a fruit of the Spirit, since we associate the latter with being generous with others, helping the poor, giving our time. However, the very act of renunciation which is inherent in martyrdom is, at its core, an expression of love – of faith and hope, but also of generosity: laying down one's life, literally, for God and sometimes even for our neighbour. Given that our most basic instinct is self-preservation, the act of surrendering one's life willingly requires extraordinary courage and a particular grace.

A martyr is a witness – the Greek word μάρτυρ (*martyr*) means witness – and while the primary act of witness is to Christ and the faith, it also serves as a witness to the power of the Holy Spirit at work within an individual. The death of a martyr is a sacrifice, an oblation, one which is united with the very sacrifice and oblation of the Lord on the cross. The martyr and Christ are intimately united since they share the one death. This also means that the martyr's offering is one with Christ's: it is part of Christ's and, as such, is part of the Lord's generous gift of himself to the Father for the salvation of the world. In his or her death, a martyr enters most fully into the very life of the Holy Trinity itself; the suffering, the sacrifice, the pouring out of one's life in love for Christ is brought into the *perichoresis*, the divine dance of God. The Church has many martyrs and in them the Holy Spirit moves across the abyss of darkness and persecution to bring order, life and light so they can endure to the end. The Lord makes great promises to those who have been with him in his trials, and endured his trials. Indeed he will confer a kingdom on them (cf. *Lk* 22:28-30); hence the image of the crown of martyrdom.

Immersed in the Spirit

Each of the martyrs reveals this work of the Spirit within him in his or her moments of trial and suffering. It is perhaps St Maximilian Kolbe who has inspired many modern men and women most by his selfless act of charity towards another man. St Maximilian, a Franciscan friar, was renowned in his lifetime for his work for Mary Immaculate. In his priestly life, he spared nothing to serve; immersed in the Spirit he had a generosity of self that defied human ability. It was his defiance of the Nazis during World War II that saw him imprisoned at the notorious concentration camp of Auschwitz. Even there his zeal could not be contained; his generous soul urged him to minister to his fellow prisoners. Though often weak and starving, he cared for them, fed them with his own rations and administered the sacraments. He made many sacrifices, took many risks within the strict and harsh regime of the camp, to bring the love of Christ to those despairing in that evil place.

But there was more to give, and Maximilian understood that. At the end of July 1941 when a prisoner escaped from the camp, ten others were chosen to die in retaliation. As one of those chosen pleaded with the deputy commander to let him live for the sake of his wife and children, Maximilian stepped forward to take his place. Confined in a bunker, a tomb for the living, Maximilian and the nine others slowly starved to death. He kept their spirits up, leading them in prayer and singing hymns, and as each died they died in his arms. After two weeks he was the only one still alive, and to finish him off the guards killed him by lethal injection; he voluntarily stretched out his arm to receive it.

In union with Christ

Another who died in that awful place also offers an example of such generosity: St Teresa Benedicta of the Cross, more commonly known by her name in the world, Edith Stein. Born into a Jewish family, she was highly intelligent, studying philosophy at university where she came under the influence of Edmund Husserl and his philosophy of phenomenology. This new branch of philosophy by its nature opened its students to the transcendent and to God and many of Husserl's students converted to Christianity. By her teens, Edith had lost her faith; now it was reawakening. Baptised a Catholic in 1922, she entered the Discalced Carmelites in Cologne in 1933, where she lived a life of prayer and study while continuing her work in philosophy.

With the Nazi persecution of the Jews, Edith, though a convert, was in danger. Fleeing Germany with her sister, Rosa, to the Carmel in Echt in the Netherlands, she was in danger again when the Nazis invaded the Netherlands in 1940. As the superior in Echt began to search for another place of refuge, Edith understood a sacrifice would have to be made and providence fell on her. Her writings reveal she knew she would perish at the hands of the Nazis and she was prepared to accept this, offering herself as a victim in union with Christ. This insight was not, it seems, the fruit of a human insight; it was revealed to her (cf. *Mt* 16:17), and she generously said yes. After all, she had been born on the Jewish feast of Yom Kippur, the Day of Atonement; it was perhaps her destiny to share in the sacrifice of the scapegoat, of the Lamb.

On 2nd August 1942, the SS arrived at her monastery gate and she and Rosa were arrested. As she was led out to a waiting car she was heard by bystanders to say, "Let us go for the sake of our people." Edith, as she noted in her writings many years before, was to be offered for the Jewish people, of which she was one and among whom she would perish in the gas chambers of Auschwitz on 9th August 1942. Edith's understanding of her death reveals the work of the Spirit, guiding her and helping her embrace the sacrifice she was called to make. When staying at Westerbork Concentration Camp before being transferred to Auschwitz she was offered a chance to escape, but she refused: to do so would be a disaster. Edith understood that if somebody intervened at this point and took away her chance to share in the fate of her brothers and sisters, that would be utter annihilation.[9]

Remaining faithful to Christ

There are others who made the same generous offering but had to endure a longer agony and whose oblation could only have been sustained by the Spirit. Among these is the Irish martyr, Blessed Margaret Bermingham. Born in Skryne, County Meath in 1515, while still a teenager she married a Dublin merchant, Bartholomew Ball. A good and faithful wife and mother, Margaret was always down-to-earth and kind. Her servants and neighbours testified to her goodness and generosity. When her husband was elected Lord Mayor of Dublin in 1553, Margaret excelled herself as first lady, her graciousness and hospitality famously enhancing her husband's term of office.

Following Queen Elizabeth I's Protestant Settlement, and as many ambitious Irish officials changed their religion to advance their careers, Margaret remained true to her Catholic faith. As persecution broke out and priests went into hiding, she set up a secret chapel in her home, offering hospitality and protection to bishops and priests as they were passing through Dublin. Her home became a centre for Catholic worship and a number of times she was arrested for recusancy.

In 1580 Margaret's son Walter was elected Lord Mayor of Dublin. He had been one of those who had converted to Protestantism, and as mayor he was determined to clamp down on recusancy in the city, setting his sights on the most notorious offender under the religious laws in the city – his mother. When

Margaret was taken into custody, she was tied down on a wooden pallet and dragged through the city streets to a cell in Dublin Castle. In her late sixties, and suffering from severe arthritis, the journey was agony for her as were the conditions of imprisonment. Walter had it communicated to her that she would remain there until she renounced Catholicism and became Protestant. When her other children objected and took action to have their mother released, Walter stood firm, informing them that he should have executed her, but had decided to be merciful and jail her instead. In fact, execution would have been more merciful. Incarcerated in a damp, underground cell with no comfort, she lasted three years before dying of her sufferings in 1584. Margaret was aware that at any moment her ordeal could be over, that all she had to do was assent to her son's demands; but she could not. She remained faithful to Christ and his Church. While many martyrs' act of generosity is made and then death is inflicted on them, Margaret had to renew her act of generosity each day, indeed many times each day as the burden of her captivity made itself felt. Her constancy cannot be explained by stubbornness; it was the work of God within her.

Conclusion

Of all the saints, the one who demonstrates most fully the life and work of the Holy Spirit within her is Our Lady, so much so that she is called the "Spouse of the Spirit". In scripture we first meet her in her home, at the moment the Archangel Gabriel came with a request from God. We see her as a humble young woman, startled by the grand form of the Archangel's address, a greeting which refers to her being full of grace (*Lk* 1:28). She is generous: seeing God's will laid out before her, and though she does not fully understand or know what will happen, she says yes. "I am the handmaid of the Lord ... let what you have said be done to me" (*Lk* 1:38): such is her total generosity to God.

Mary's openness to the will of God and her willingness to allow the Spirit to possess her in grace is akin to a marriage and it makes her fruitful. The fruits of the Holy Spirit are truly present and at work within her, transforming her to an extraordinary degree not only for her role as Mother of God but also for her vocation as the first and most faithful of all the disciples of her Son. Of all the fruits, that of generosity marks her vocation in a singular way.

Mary was called to give, and God in his goodness prepared her for this role. As Mother she gave birth to the Son: she gave God his human nature, his flesh. She fed him at her breast and raised him, introducing him to human society. She accompanied him in his public ministry, in prayer rather than physically beside him. But when the moment of the sacrifice comes, she is at his side, enduring the pain of martyrdom in a unique way as she stands with her Son in his suffering. Her motherly heart pierced, she too is poured out as an oblation in sorrow in union with her Son. The painful deposition of her Son's body from the cross, as it is laid upon her knees, makes her an altar of sacrifice as she embraces and then offers to the Father the life she brought into the world. The Pietà is the image of Mary's complete oblation to God, revealing the depths of her generosity. As the prophecy laments: was there any sorrow like unto hers (cf. *Lm* 1:12)? In all of this, Mary, fruitful Virgin, is sustained by the fruitfulness of the Spirit's work within her.

As followers of Christ we are to look to Mary and see in her the way of Christian discipleship. While we may try to qualify our hesitancy with reference to the unique graces she received – her being conceived immaculate, for example, we cannot forget that Mary made a decision in the full light of day to give all to God. While the Spirit guided and sustained her, she was still free to say no, to hold back. Instead, she chose to be generous with God, and that opened her up to the power of the Spirit and his triumph within. As her story in scripture begins with an invitation and a response, so does ours. God speaks to us, he seeks to plant the seed within us and through his Spirit make it grow; but it falls to us to say yes or no – to be generous or not. If we say yes, if we are generous, then God will open his stores and share with us his treasures. He will sustain us for our particular vocation, providing what we cannot provide but need; and he will transform us and sanctify us.

Generosity is a fruit that is given so we can fulfil Christ's command to love God with all our heart, all our mind and all our strength (*Mk* 12:30), and love our neighbour with a selfless and Christ-like love. It is no wonder that this call to give love to God is the Jewish profession of faith, the *Shemà* (*Dt* 6:5): it is meant to be the expression of ours.

Appendix: Examen

An examen is a prayerful reflection on one's life or day, a spiritual exercise to assist us in our growth in the Christian life, in virtue and in holiness. This brief examen is designed to help you reflect on the matters discussed in this booklet in the context of the events of your day with a view to allowing the Holy Spirit to direct you and find space within you so his fruit of generosity may become a guide for your life.

The fruit of generosity

- Have I been generous with my time and made space for the prayer of the heart each day?

- Have I allowed the Anointing of the Sacrament of Confirmation to open my heart to the Spirit?

- Have I invoked the Spirit as I begin my prayer and all the actions of my day?

- Have I tried to abandon my discernment and decisions to the Holy Spirit?

- Have I looked to events of my day/life and tried to orient them in a manner to allow the Holy Spirit to work within me and within them?

Material generosity

- Have I tried to cultivate a spirit of generosity within myself?

- Have I neglected my duty to those around me who are in need?

- Have I given alms to the poor?

- Have I let personal pride, differences or feelings get in the way of helping others who are in need?

- Have I exercised due prudence and care with regard to my almsgiving?

The gift of self

- Have I offered my life and gifts to the service of God and his Church?

- Have I been generous with those in need of time and attention?

- Have I avoided people for any reason?

- Have I chosen my welfare over the welfare of others in need?

- Do I harbour ill will towards others? Have I refused to forgive those who have offended me?

Martyrdom

- Have I preferred comfort to sacrifices?

- Have I nurtured a selflessness which shifts my attention from myself to God and others?

- Have I embraced my cross with generosity?

- Have I prayed for strength to endure to the end?

- Am I prepared to stand by my faith and even endure hardship and mockery?

- Am I prepared to die for Christ, forgiving those who kill me with a generous heart and submitting humbly, trusting in God?

Prayer for generosity

Lord, teach me to be generous.
Teach me to serve you as you deserve:
to give and not to count the cost,
to fight and not to heed the wounds,
to toil and not to seek for rest,
to labour and not to ask for reward,
save that of knowing that I do your will.

St Ignatius of Loyola

Endnotes

[1] See *Living Fruitfully: Self-Control*, Catholic Truth Society, 2017, "Fruits of the Holy Spirit", pp. 10-17.

[2] *Catechism of the Catholic Church*, § 1832.

[3] Tertullian, *Apologeticum*, Chapter 39, 7. The actual quotation, referring to how the Romans observed the Christians, is: "'Look,' they say, 'how they love one another' (for they themselves hate one another); 'and how they are ready to die for each other' (for they themselves are readier to kill each other)."

[4] St Gregory Nazianzen, *First Letter to Cledonius* (Letter 101).

[5] Pope St John Paul II, *Dives in Misericordia*, (1980) § 13.

[6] Blessed James Alberione's own account of his experience, related in Rev. Stephen Lamera, SSP, *James Alberione: "Marvel of Our Times"*, Paulines Publishing House, Pasay, Philippines, 1977.

[7] St Faustina Kowalska, *Diary: Divine Mercy in My Soul*, 9.

[8] John 15:13.

[9] Cf. Joanne Mosley, *Edith Stein: Modern Saint and Martyr*, Paulist Press, Mahwah, NJ, 2006, pp. 43-52.

Living Fruitfully: Chastity

Fr John Mckeever

"If you would be happy, be chaste."

This title addresses the provocative and misunderstood subject of chastity. Too often considered an exclusively 'religious' option, the author makes the case for chastity, showing that as a Christian virtue, we are all called to lead a chaste life in keeping with our particular state of life: whether married, single, ordained, lay, young or old.

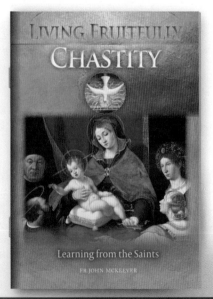

PA44   ISBN: 978 1 78469 200 1

Living Fruitfully: Joy

Mgr Paul Grogan

"Joy is not merely a positive emotion which can be displaced by negative ones, but a settled attribute in the soul."

By drawing on examples of saints like St Bonaventure and St Paul, the author helps us consider three ways we can experience joy: remaining close to Jesus in prayer; speaking of Jesus to others and following Jesus.

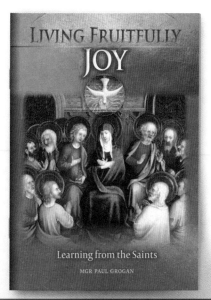

PA42   ISBN: 978 1 78469 191 2

Living Fruitfully: Self-Control

Fr John S Hogan

"It is God's intention that you and I may act upon what the Spirit seeks to give us so we may be sustained and transformed; strong and holy; fit for mission and for the kingdom of heaven."

This title examines the fruit of self-control illustrating how the saints were a model for this attribute, and givine examples of how self-control might be demonstrated in daily life. It concludes with a series of questions to help us examine the presence of the fruit in our own lives, moving us beyond reflection and discussion to application.

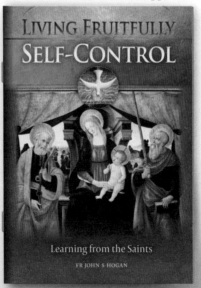

PA35   ISBN 978 1 78469 172 1

Has this book helped you?
Spread the word!

@CTSpublishers

/CTSpublishers

ctscatholiccompass.org

Let us know!
marketing@ctsbooks.org
+44 (0)207 640 0042

Learn, love, live your faith.
www.CTSbooks.org